MAKING SENSE OF PERCENT

BY MARGARET THOMAS

illustrated by Gary Hoover

cover illustrations by Gary Hoover

Publisher
Instructional Fair • TS Denison
Grand Rapids, Michigan 49544

ISBN:1-56822-627-6
Making Sense of Percent
Copyright © 1998 by Instructional Fair • TS Denison
2400 Turner Avenue NW
Grand Rapids, Michigan 49544

TABLE OF CONTENTS

ABOUT THIS BOOK

Making Sense of Percent provides the teacher with strategies, activities, and games for the instruction and review of percent concepts. The strategies and activities incorporate the use of physical models for the representation of percent quantities. Area and linear models are used not only to introduce and reinforce the percent concepts, but also to solve problems involving percents. Reliance on phrases such as "two places to the right" and "is over of" is deemphasized. Students are encouraged to visualize the percent quantity using static and variable models such as 100-unit squares and elastic strips.

The book includes four sections: Percent Models, Percent Computations, Percent and Common Sense, and Percent Games. Answers are provided. Although several activities complement one another, their order of presentation is left to the discretion of the teacher, as the activities can be used in any order.

Each activity has a teacher introduction which includes the topic, materials list, procedures, and comments. Teacher strategies are included along with discussion suggestions. Additional math concepts such as area, evens and odds, primes and composites, and the coordinate grid are included. The reasonableness of an answer is emphasized throughout the book. Use of estimation is encouraged. Where appropriate, comments concerning calculator differences are mentioned.

Percent Models

Percent is one of the most commonly used math concepts. Almost every newspaper and magazine present information using percents. It is not uncommon to find adults who cannot estimate or calculate sale prices, discounts, tax rates, and tips. Many students confess being confused about percent and not understanding the basics of percent computations: "Should I move the decimal to the right or to the left?" "If an item that is marked '50% off' is an additional 25% off, doesn't that mean it is 75% off?" Some of the confusion is due to the rote processes students use to perform percent computations in school. Instruction should emphasize context and reasonableness of answers. Models should be used that enable students to visualize and understand concepts pertaining to percents.

Several models can be used to help students visualize percent quantities. The 100-unit square, rectangular bars, and plate circle graphs are models that use area to show and determine percent quantities. The ladder bar and the elastic strip are two models that use linear measure to demonstrate and calculate percents. Proportion mnemonics such as "is over of" and equation setups such as "pb = a" can be used with the models to calculate percent quantities. Each of the stated models is presented and explained with suggested activities in this publication.

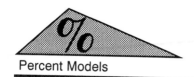

SHADY PERCENTS

Activity: Students estimate the percent of a square that is shaded. A transparent 100-unit square is used to figure the actual percent.

Materials: activity sheet for each student
transparent 100-unit square for each student or small group
See the black line master of the 100-unit squares on "What's the Percent? I & II."

100-unit square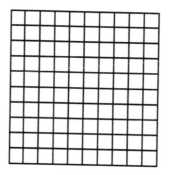

Comments: Students should be encouraged to use 10%, 25%, 50%, 75%, and 90% as reference values. Emphasize that a 100-unit square is used because *percent* means *per hundred*. Therefore, 10% is 10 *squares per 100 squares*. It may be necessary to point out to students that the transparent square does not need to be placed exactly over the given square. It can be aligned with the shaded region to make counting the unit squares easier, since the total area of the region given is the same as the 100-unit square.

Make certain that copies of the activity sheet and the transparencies are made on the same machine. Then any enlargement from the copy process will be the same for both.

This activity lends itself to small-group and class discussion.

SHADY PERCENTS

Estimate the percent shaded in each figure. Use a transparent 100-unit square to find the actual percent.

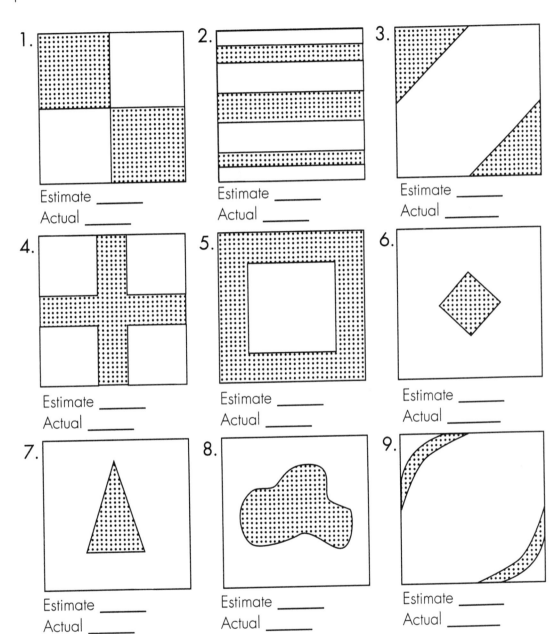

1. Estimate _____
   Actual _____

2. Estimate _____
   Actual _____

3. Estimate _____
   Actual _____

4. Estimate _____
   Actual _____

5. Estimate _____
   Actual _____

6. Estimate _____
   Actual _____

7. Estimate _____
   Actual _____

8. Estimate _____
   Actual _____

9. Estimate _____
   Actual _____

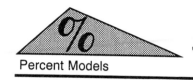
ESTIMATING PERCENTS I & II

Activity: Students estimate the percent of regions and values using given reference percents: 1%, 25%, 50%, 75%, 100%, and 150%.

Materials: one activity sheet per student

Comments: To prepare for the activities, review the reference percents.

Discuss fractions that approximate 0, ¼, ½, ¾, 1, and ³⁄₂ by comparing the relative sizes of the numerator and denominator. The smaller the numerator is compared to the denominator, the closer a fraction is to 0. Likewise, the closer the numerator is to half of the denominator, the closer the fraction is to ½. If the numerator is almost equal to the denominator, the fraction is close to 1.

Discuss equivalent and approximate values:
1% is close to 0. The indicated quantity is very small compared to the whole amount, such as 1 to 100, 3 to 275, 25 to 2,100.
25% equals ¼. The indicated quantity is substantially less than half of the whole amount, such as 5 to 20, 9 to 30, and 40 to 150.
50% equals ½. The indicated quantity approximates half of the whole amount, such as 12 to 24, 30 to 65, and 215 to 400.
75% equals ¾. The indicated quantity is substantially more than half of the whole amount, such as 30 to 40, 7 to 10, and 240 to 300.
100% equals 1. The indicated quantity approximates the whole amount, such as 50 to 50, 24 to 25, 195 to 200.
150% equals ³⁄₂ which equals 1½. The indicated quantity is substantially greater than the original quantity (whole amount), such as 9 to 6, 30 to 20, and 375 to 250.

It is important that students are able to identify the indicated quantity (amount) and the whole quantity (base) in each situation.

"Estimating Percents II" uses vertical bars and leads to the use of the ladder bar method for solving percent problems.

ESTIMATING PERCENTS I

Estimate the following quantities using the percents given. Do not calculate exact amounts.

1%   25%   75%   100%

50%   150%

1. The shaded region: _____

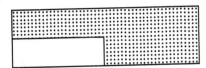

2. The shaded region: _____

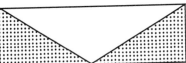

3. The unshaded region: _____

4. The unshaded region: _____

5. Twelve of the 22 students are girls.   _____

6. What percent of 62 is 46?   _____

7. Three of the 297 students were state winners.   _____

8. Last year the jacket cost $70. Now it costs $100.   _____

9. The Jacobsons left a $5.00 tip for a $22.74 bill.   _____

10. Jan scored 40 out of 40 on the science test.   _____

 # ESTIMATING PERCENTS II

Let  represent 100%. Estimate the following quantities using the percents given.

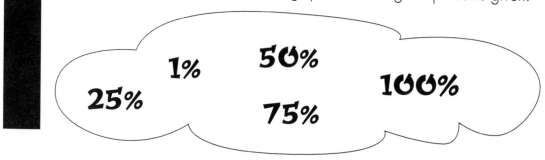

25%   1%   50%   75%   100%

1. _____   2. _____   3. _____   4. _____   5. _____

   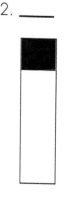      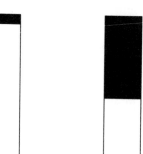   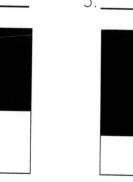

Shade each bar to show the given percent.

6. 40%   7. 20%   8. 90%   9. 10%   10. 70%

11. Write a math statement for which the quantity shown in #6 would be an estimate. For example, #1: There were 22 girls in the class of 40 students.

_____

_____

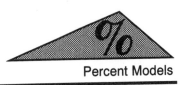

NUMBER CHART PERCENT

Activity: The students use a 100-number chart (numbers from 1 through 100) to estimate the percent of the numbers meeting given criteria.

Materials: 100-number chart per student or transparency of 100-number chart for the overhead

Comments: This activity reinforces concepts of percent such as "number out of 100" and the area model. It also reviews number properties and terminology. The number properties and terms can be adapted to meet any number concepts needing review.

NUMBER CHART PERCENT

1	2	3	4	5	6	7	8	9	10
11	12	13	14	15	16	17	18	19	20
21	22	23	24	25	26	27	28	29	30
31	32	33	34	35	36	37	38	39	40
41	42	43	44	45	46	47	48	49	50
51	52	53	54	55	56	57	58	59	60
61	62	63	64	65	66	67	68	69	70
71	72	73	74	75	76	77	78	79	80
81	82	83	84	85	86	87	88	89	90
91	92	93	94	95	96	97	98	99	100

Estimate the numbers 1 through 100 that

1. are even numbers. _____

2. are multiples of 5. _____

3. are multiples of 9. _____

4. contain digits with a sum of 9. _____

5. are prime numbers. _____

6. are composite numbers. _____

7. contain 2 as a digit. _____

8. contain only even digits. _____

9. contain only odd digits. _____

10. contain an even and an odd digit. _____

SHADY PICTURES I & II

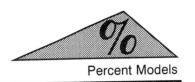

Activity: Students plot and connect points on a coordinate grid. Then they shade the resulting picture and determine the percent of the grid included in the picture.

Materials: activity sheet for each student

Comments: "Shady Pictures I" uses only the first quadrant. The coordinates range from 0 to 10.

"Shady Pictures II" uses all four quadrants. The coordinates range from -5 to 5.

The activity presents a geometric representation of percent while reviewing plotting points, negative integers, areas of rectangles and triangles.

As a follow-up activity, have students create their own pictures and list the points. Have them exchange their lists with a partner, plot the partner's points, and determine percents.

 SHADY PICTURES I

Plot the points. Connect them in order. Shade the picture and determine the percent of the grid that is shaded.

1. (4,0),   (4,1),   (2,1),   (3,2),   (3,3),   (4,4),   (4,8),   (5,9),
    (6,8),   (6,4),   (7,3),   (7,2),   (8,1),   (6,1),   (6,0),   (4,0)

_____ %

2. (3,1),   (3,3),   (2,2),   (1,3),   (4,6),   (4,4),   (7,4),   (8,5),
    (8,4),   (7,3),   (7,1),   (6,1),   (6,2),   (4,2),   (4,1),   (3,1)

_____ %

SHADY PICTURES II

Plot the points. Connect them in order. Shade the picture and determine the percent of the grid that is shaded.

1. (0,3),   (2,3),   (2,1),   (5,1),   (5,-1),   (4,-1),   (3,-2),   (2,-2),
    (1,-1),   (-1,-1),   (-2,-2),   (-3,-2),   (-4,-1),   (-4,1),   (-2,2),   (0,3)

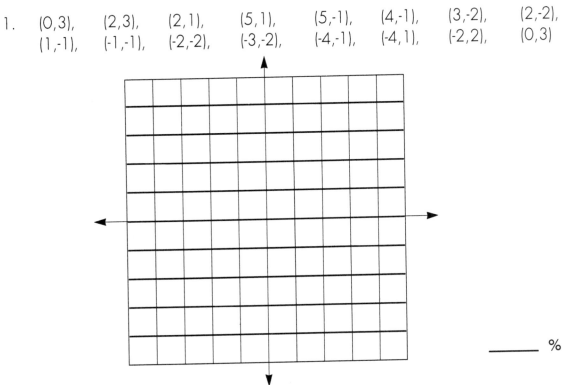

_____ %

2. (-1,1),   (-1,2),   (0,3),   (-2,3),   (-4,2),   (-2,2),   (-2,1),   (-2.5,0),
    (-3,-1),   (-2,-2),   (1,-2),   (2,0),   (2,1),   (3,3),   (1,3),   (1,1)   (-1,1)

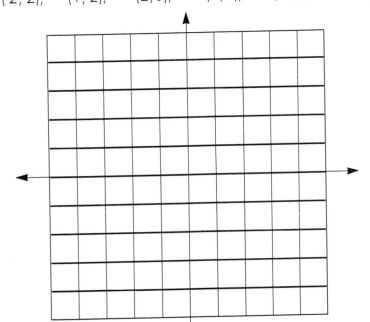

_____ %

IF2649 Making Sense of Percent

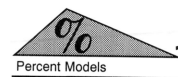

WHAT'S THE PERCENT? I & II

Activity: Students use a 100-unit square to determine the percent when given the part and the whole amount. "What's the Percent? I" uses base numbers of 10 and 20. "What's the Percent? II" uses bases of 5, 25, and 50.

Materials: activity sheet for each student
transparent 100-unit square for each student (see below)

Comments: Students shade the number of small sections of the given square to model the problem. Then they place the transparent 100-unit grid on top to find what percent is shaded.

> Example:　　8 is what percent of 10?
> Shade 8 of the 10 sections.
> Place 100-unit grid on top.
> 80 squares cover the shaded region.
> Therefore, 8 is 80% of 10.

The activities use the area concept of percent—What area of the 100-unit grid is shaded? The bases used are factors of 100. A related activity is to write each problem as a proportion and calculate the equivalent fraction.

> Example:　　8 is what percent of 10?
> $8/10 = n/100$
> $n = 80$
> 80%

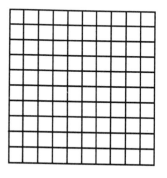 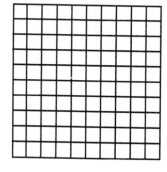 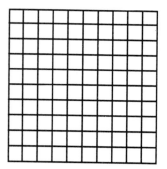

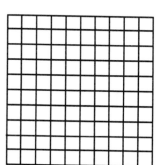 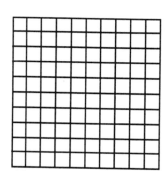 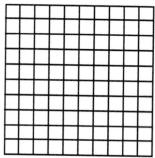

Name _____

WHAT'S THE PERCENT? 1 %

Shade each square according to the amount given in each problem. Place the 100-unit square on top to determine the percent.

1. 8 is what percent of 10? _____

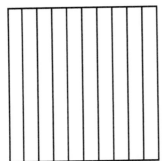

2. 3 is what percent of 10? _____

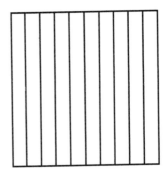

3. 7 is what percent of 10? _____

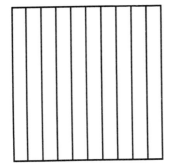

4. 8 is what percent of 20? _____

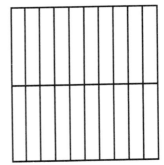

5. 13 is what percent of 20? _____

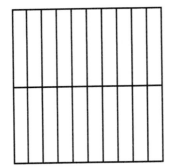

6. 17 is what percent of 20? _____

Bonus: How would you show "37 is what percent of 20?" Hint: Use problem number 6.

WHAT'S THE PERCENT? II

Shade each square according to the amount given in each problem. Place the 100-unit square on top to determine the percent.

1. 3 is what percent of 5? _____

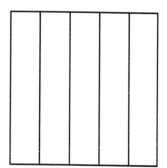

2. 1 is what percent of 5? _____

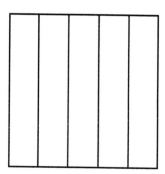

3. 5 is what percent of 25? _____

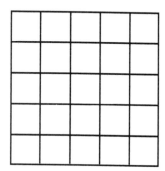

4. 17 is what percent of 25? _____

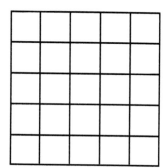

5. 20 is what percent of 50? _____

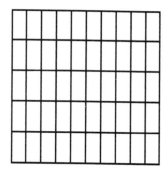

6. 35 is what percent of 50? _____

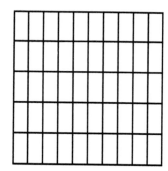

Bonus: How would you show "85 is what percent of 50?" Hint: Use problem 6.

Activity: Students in pairs or small groups use base squares to determine the amount that is a given percent of a number.

Materials: activity sheet for each student
transparency of base squares for each group (see below)

Comments: Since transparencies of the base squares are to be used, students should work in pairs or small groups to reduce the number of transparencies needed.

Students shade the given percent of the 100-unit square. Then place the appropriate transparent base square on top to find how many regions have been shaded.

Example: What is 20% of 10?
Shade 20 squares of 100-unit square.
Place the 10-unit base square on top.
Two sections cover the shaded region.
Therefore, 2 is 20% of 10.

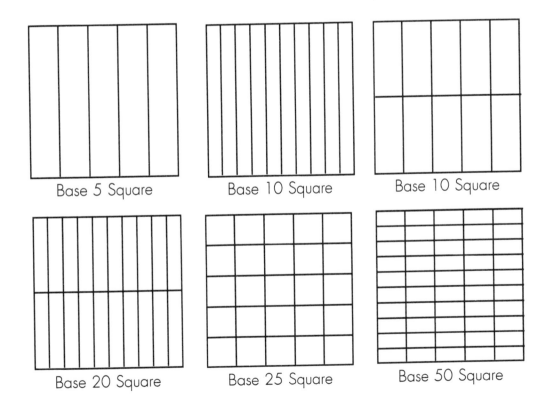

Base 5 Square   Base 10 Square   Base 10 Square

Base 20 Square   Base 25 Square   Base 50 Square

 # FINDING THE PERCENT OF A NUMBER

Shade each 100-unit square to show the given percent. Use an appropriate base square to determine the amount.

1. What is 20% of 10? _____

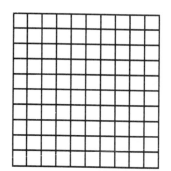

2. What is 60% of 20? _____

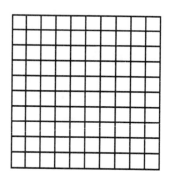

3. What is 35% of 20? _____

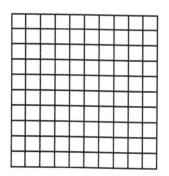

4. What is 40% of 5? _____

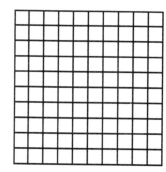

5. What is 20% of 25? _____

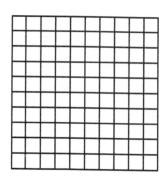

6. What is 46% of 50? _____

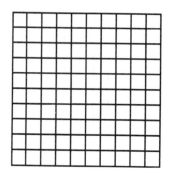

Bonus: How would you show "What is 120% of 25?" Hint: Use problem 5.

PLATE CIRCLE GRAPHS

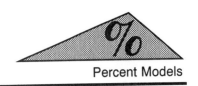

Activity: Students work in pairs or small groups to identify ratios, show equivalent areas on a circle graph, and determine the related percent values.

Materials: For each pair or group of students:
10 two-color counters (painted medium or large lima beans)
1 plate circle graph (two plates each)
1 tally sheet (notebook paper)

Comments: Construction:

Counters:
To make two-sided counters, spread medium to large lima beans out on newspaper and spray paint one side. Paint at least ten beans for each group of students. (The natural bean color will be the second color. Painting both sides different colors can be messy and time-consuming.) Count out sets of ten beans into bags or envelopes. If possible, use the same color for one part of the plate circle graphs.

Plate Circle Graphs:
Each plate circle graph is made from two different-colored plates. Thin plastic six- or seven-inch plates are easy to use. Cut a slit from the center to the edge (a radius cut) in each plate. Mesh two plates together, one of each color. The plates can then be rotated to represent the comparison of two quantities.

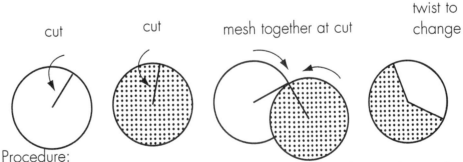

Procedure:
Give each pair or group of students counters and a plate circle graph. Have the groups count out the desired number of counters for the activity. The example shown uses five counters for percent values of 0%, 20%, 40%, 60%, 80%, and 100%.

PLATE CIRCLE GRAPHS (cont.)

1) One student tosses the counters, gives the number of each color, and states a corresponding ratio.

2) The other student shows the relationship on the plate circle graph and determines equivalent percent relationships.

3) The first student or third student serves as the recorder and writes the equivalent statements.

4) Repeat steps 1-3, rotating jobs. The number of counters used can be changed to reinforce other percent values.

The recorder for each group can then relate the information to the class or the record sheets for each group can be collected.

Example:

1) Toss 5 beans:

Give the number of each color: "2 red, 3 beige"

State ratio: "The ratio of red to beige is 2 to 3 or 2/3."
"The ratio of red to all is 2/5. The ratio of beige to all is 3/5."

2) Show the relationship on the plate circle graph:

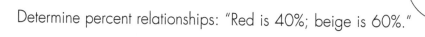

Determine percent relationships: "Red is 40%; beige is 60%."

3) Record equivalent statements: ⅖ red = 40% red
⅗ beige = 60% beige

Students who have difficulty showing the relationship on the circle graphs should be encouraged to space the beans equally apart around the edge of the plate, matching the color of the bean with the corresponding plate color.

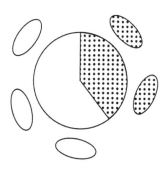

PLATE CIRCLE GRAPHS

Trial #1

Number of counters:_____   Record Color 1:_____   Record Color 2:_____

Toss the counters.   Number of Color 1:_____   Number of Color 2:_____

Ratio of Color 1 to Color 2: _____   Ratio of Color 2 to Color 1:_____

Show ratios on plate circle graph and sketch below: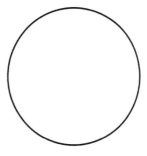

Ratio of Color 1 to all: _____   Ratio of Color 2 to all: _____

Give equivalent percents:

Color 1 to all is_____ = _____%   Color 2 to all is_____ = _____%

Trial #2

Number of counters:_____   Record Color 1:_____   Record Color 2:_____

Toss the counters.   Number of Color 1:_____   Number of Color 2:_____

Ratio of Color 1 to Color 2: _____   Ratio of Color 2 to Color 1:_____

Show ratios on plate circle graph and sketch below: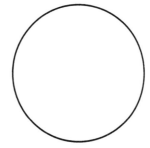

Ratio of Color 1 to all: _____   Ratio of Color 2 to all: _____

Give equivalent percents:

Color 1 to all is_____ = _____%   Color 2 to all is_____ = _____%

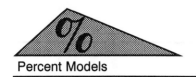
Activity: "Circle Graphs I": Students estimate the relative size of regions of a circle as a percent. "Circle Graphs II": Students use given data to calculate percents and draw circle graphs.

Materials: activity sheet for each student
optional: transparent circle protractor for class discussion

Comments: If possible, use a transparent circle protractor and discuss the relationship between degree measure and percent. The activities require students to estimate percent regions, so students should realize that 25% is ¼ of a circle, which is 90 degrees. Other reference percents to discuss and demonstrate with the overhead protractor include 10% (36 degrees), 50% (180 degrees), and 75% (270 degrees). The "Circle Graph I" activity could be expanded to include estimating the number of degrees in each region.

For "Circle Graph II," review that p = a/b. Percent equals the part (amount) divided by the whole quantity (base).

Example: R $8,000 out of $25,000 becomes
p = 8,000/25,000 so p = 32%,
so approximately ⅓ of the circle should be labeled R.

Circle Graphs I

For each circle, estimate the percent of each region.

1.
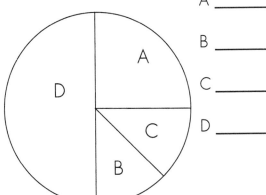

A _____
B _____
C _____
D _____

2.
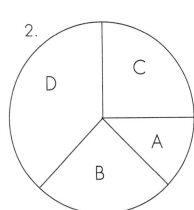

A _____
B _____
C _____
D _____

3.
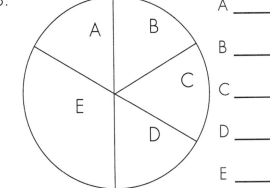

A _____
B _____
C _____
D _____
E _____

4.
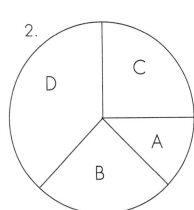

A _____
B _____
C _____
D _____
E _____

5.
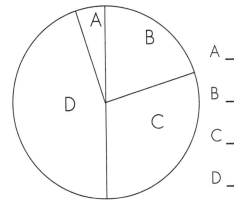

A _____
B _____
C _____
D _____

6.
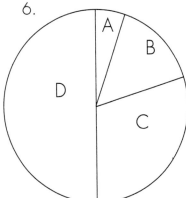

A _____
B _____
C _____
D _____

21

CIRCLE GRAPHS II

For each problem, calculate the percent for each quantity and label the circle graphs.

1.

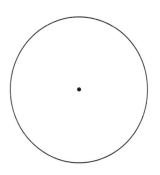

2.

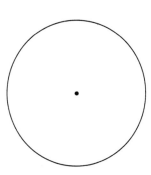

50 students: A. 15 A's _____ 200 pets: D. 90 dogs _____

                  B. 20 B's _____   C. 60 cats _____

                  C. 10 C's _____   F. 30 fish _____

                  D.   5 D's _____   H. 20 mice _____

3.

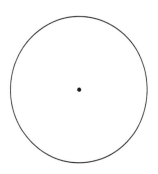

4.

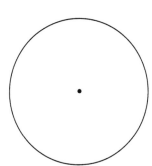

$25,000 income: R. $8,000 rent _____   300 juice cans O. 168 orange _____

                      T. $5,000 taxes _____   A. 60 apple _____

                      F. $4,000 food _____   G. 45 grape _____

                      C. $3,000 car _____   P. 18 prune _____

                      S. $5,000 misc./_____   B. 9 blends _____

                           savings

Bar Graphs Into Circle Graphs

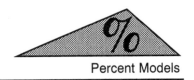

Activity: Students make a bar graph and use it to construct a circle graph. The data should be of mutually exclusive events.

Materials: per student or small group of students:
activity sheet
scissors
colored pencils or crayons
tape
optional: transparency of bar graph for class discussion

Procedure:

1. Pose a question to the class and collect data. Suggested topics include: number of pets, number of brothers and sisters, favorite food, ice-cream flavor, etc.

   Optional: provide data to the students.

2. Plot the data on the bar graph. Hint: Leave a space between bars.

3. Cut out the bars. Leave an extra space at the end of each bar.

4. Tape the bars together end to end. Use the extra space to overlap and tape. Tape the end of the last bar to the start of the first so the colors face outward.

5. Form a circle and center it on the circle graph.

6. Mark off arcs on the circle corresponding to the ends of each bar.

7. Draw radii from the center to the arc. Label regions—instant circle graph!

8. Repeat for the second graph or assign it.

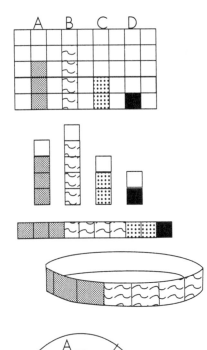

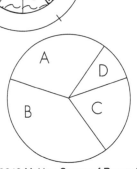

BAR GRAPHS INTO CIRCLE GRAPHS

Use the bar graphs below to make circle graphs. Label each region.

1.

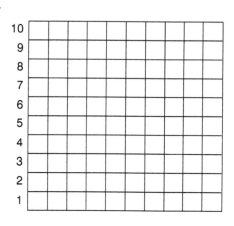

2.

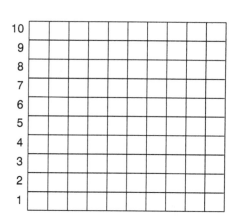

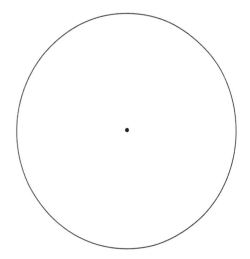

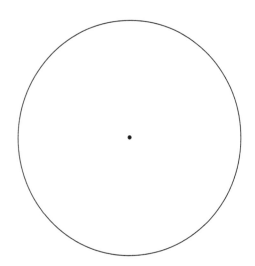

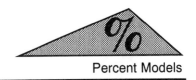
Bar Graphs and Circle Graphs

Activity: Students use data given in percent form first to determine which type of graph to use (bar or circle) and then to complete the graphs using the data.

Materials: activity sheet per student
ruler
circle protractor (optional)

Comments: A circle graph should be used only when the data represent mutually exclusive events. The circle represents 100% so the data totals 100% (see circle graph example below). In a bar graph, each bar can represent 100% of each segment of the data so the sum of the stated percents can be greater than 100%. A bar graph is also used when the events are not mutually exclusive events (see bar graph example below).

Circle Graph

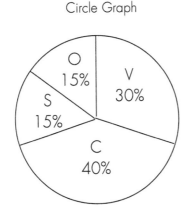

Bar Graph

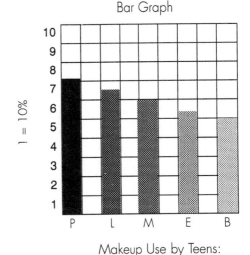

Favorite Flavor:

vanilla	30%
chocolate	40%
strawberry	15%
others	15%
total	100%

Makeup Use by Teens:

polish	72%
lipstick	67%
mascara	60%
eye shadow	55%
blush	50%
total	greater than 100%

In this activity, students are given data and they need to identify the data appropriate for the circle graphs. Students need to identify the problems that have data that can be displayed on a circle graph. The bar graphs are used for the rest of the problems.

Bar Graphs and Circle Graphs

Identify which data could be displayed on a circle graph. Use the circles to graph the data. Label the regions. Use the grids to make bar graphs of the data of the other problems. Label the axes and bars.

1. Diet concerns:

Age:	18-24	20%
	25-34	28%
	35-49	30%
	50-64	38%
	65+	43%

American Dietetic Assoc. BKG Youth/Nintendo

2. Parental help with homework per week:

Hours:	none	24%
	1-4	32%
	5+	44%

3. Airplane reading:

airline magazine	56%
own magazine	46%
book	41%
work/study items	17%

World Airline Entertainment Assoc.

4. Family income spent for food:

India	53%
China	48%
Mexico	32%
Japan	18%
USA	10%

ACA Education Foundation

5. Pasta favorites:

spaghetti	45%
macaroni & cheese	30%
noodles	15%
lasagna	10%

6. Rewards employees want:

cash	58%
extra vacation	22%
travel award	8%
gift certificate	2%
other	10%

American Express/Michaelson & Assoc.

_____

_____

_____

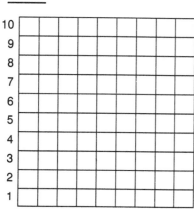

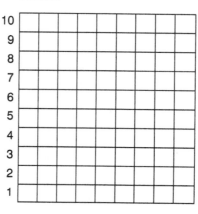

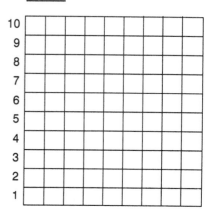

_____

_____

_____

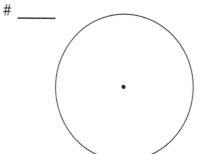

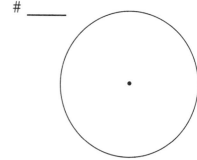

VARIABLE PERCENT

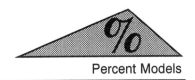

Activity: Students work in pairs to label an elastic strip (or rubber band) as a model for percent relationships. Students use the strip with number lines to solve percent problems.

Materials: activity sheet for each student.
elastic strip or rubber band (about 8-9 cm long and 1-2 cm wide) for each pair of students

Comments: Percent quantities vary according to the size of the base value. Some students have difficulty with this concept. For instance, 40 percent is not a set amount, it varies according to the base. Forty percent of a large number is a large amount and 40 percent of a small number is a small amount.

The elastic strip is a linear model like the horizontal ladder bar which varies in length according to the base quantity.

Have students work in pairs. One student stretches the strip along the number line given. The other student marks the band in 10 equal units which will correspond to 0-100% in 10% units. The students use the strip to locate points on number lines to solve percent problems.

Examples:
1) Locate the point 40% from S to B:

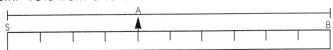

Stretch the strip from S(0) to B(100) and mark an A on the line at the 40 mark on the strip.

2) Determine what percent point A is from S to B:

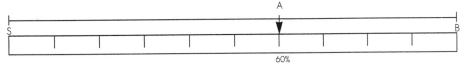

Stretch the strip from S(0) to B(100) and note that A is above the 60 mark on the strip.

3) Determine the length of the line of which S to A is 40%:

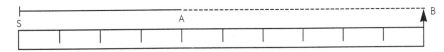

Stretch the strip from S(0) so that the 40 mark is at A, mark a B above the 100 mark, and finish the line.

VARIABLE PERCENT

Stretch the elastic strip or rubber band along the number line below. Mark the strip 0 through 10. Each mark will correspond to 10%.

On each line, mark point A the given percent of the distance from point S to point B. Stretch your elastic strip along each line below, placing 0 on point S and 10 on point B.

1. 50% S _____B

2. 80% S _____B

3. 40% S _____B

4. 20% S _____B

Approximate the percent of the way point A is from point S to point B.

5. S _____ A _____B

6. S _____ A _____B

7. S_____ A _____B

8. S _____ A___B

Locate point B so that point A is the given percent from point S. Stretch your elastic strip along each line below placing 0 on point S and the mark corresponding to the given percent on point A.

9. 70% S_____A - - - - - - - - - - - - -

10. 50% S_____A - - - - - - - - - - - - -

11. 90% S_____A - - - -

12. 30% S_____A - - - - - - - - - - - - - - - - -

LADDER BARS

Activity: Students use vertical bars to estimate the missing part of a percent problem. The bars can be used with the proportion method or equation method to calculate exact quantities.

Materials: activity sheet of ladder bars or student-produced bars

Procedure: A vertical bar or *ladder* is drawn. The bar can be lightly scored in quarters to aid in estimation (see Bar 1). On the left edge, the percent quantities are written, 0% on top, 100% on the bottom. If a percent (p) is given, its location is estimated compared to the 0% and 100% and a horizontal line is drawn (see Bar 2). On the right edge, 0 is marked at the top to correspond to 0%. If the whole (b) is given, it is written on the right side opposite the 100%, and the amount (a) can be estimated from the horizontal line drawn from the given percent (see Bar 3).

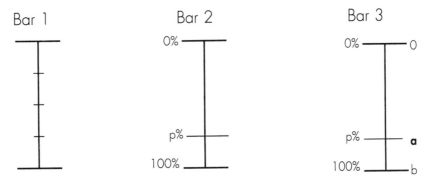

If the part (a) is given, it is located on the right side opposite the percent and the whole (b) can be estimated (see Bar 4). If the percent is not given, the whole (b) is located opposite the 100% and the part is located on the right side. A horizontal line is drawn and the percent can be estimated (see Bar 5). The ladder bar can be extended for problems involving percents greater than 100% (see Bar 6).

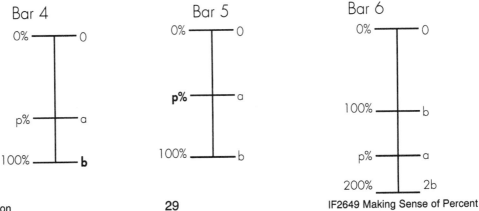

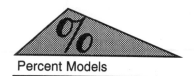
Examples:

Estimate 30% of 40.   Estimate 75% of what number is 60.   Estimate 40 out of 50 is what %?

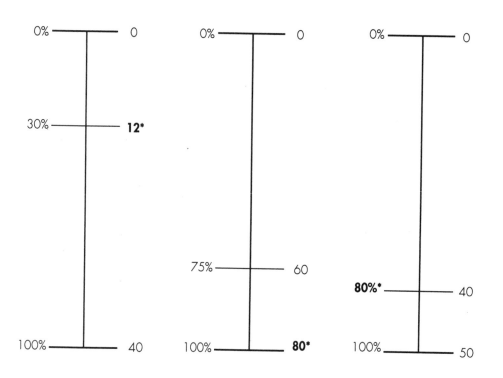

0% — 0

30% — **12***

100% — 40

0% — 0

75% — 60

100% — **80***

0% — 0

80%* — 40

100% — 50

* indicates the estimated answer.

Comments:

The ladder bars should be demonstrated using several examples, as given above. Any percent problems can be assigned for students to label ladder bars and estimate the location of the solution.

LADDER BARS AND PROPORTIONS

Since the ladder bars are written with 0% on top and 100% on the bottom, they can be used with the proportion method to solve percent problems. Percent over 100 ($\%/100$) is the left side of the ladder bar and the part over whole ($\frac{a}{b}$) is the right side of the ladder bar. Simply write the percent over 100 (left side of the bar) equal to the part over the whole (right side of the bar). The estimated location of the solution on the bar is a check for the reasonableness of the solution.

Examples:

What is 30% of 27?

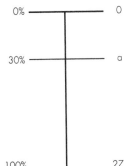

65% of what number is 42?

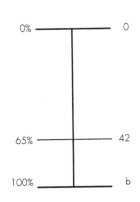

75 is what % of 90?

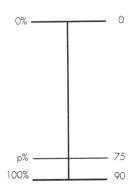

$$\frac{30}{100} = \frac{a}{27}$$

$$30 \times 27 = 100a$$

$$\frac{810}{100} = a$$

$$8.1 = a$$

$$\frac{65}{100} = \frac{42}{b}$$

$$65b = 42 \times 100$$

$$b = \frac{4200}{65}$$

$$b = 64.6$$

$$\frac{p}{100} = \frac{75}{90}$$

$$90b = 7500$$

$$b = \frac{7500}{90}$$

$$b = 83.3\%$$

Problems:

Use the ladder bars to estimate the location of the answer. Then set up the proportion and solve.

What is 60% of 95?

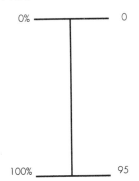

35% of what number is 42?

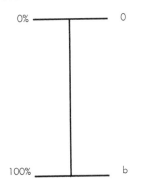

24 is what % of 64?

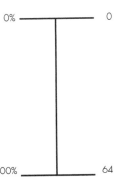

%△ LADDER BARS AND EQUATIONS

Since the ladder bars are written with the percents on the left, they lend themselves to writing equations of the form $pb = a$ (percent times base = amount).

Examples:

The discount on a $80.00 coat is 20%. Find the discount. _____

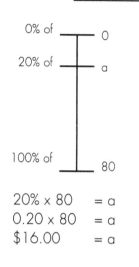

$$20\% \times 80 = a$$
$$0.20 \times 80 = a$$
$$\$16.00 = a$$

Kelly earned $300 as a 6% commission on sales. How much did Kelly sell? _____

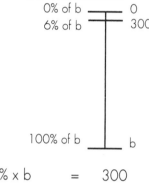

$$6\% \times b = 300$$

$$\frac{0.06 \times b}{0.06} = \frac{300}{0.06}$$
$$b = \$5,000$$

Jo should eat 2000 calories. She ate 2400 calories. What percent of the diet calories did she eat? _____

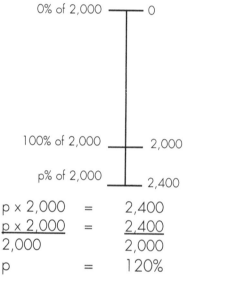

$$p \times 2,000 = 2,400$$
$$\frac{p \times 2,000}{2,000} = \frac{2,400}{2,000}$$
$$p = 120\%$$

Problems:

Use the ladder bars to estimate the location of the answer. Then write equations and solve.

Mrs. Allen wants to leave a 15% tip. The bill came to $16.00. How much should she leave? _____

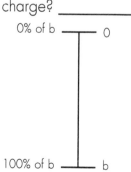

Saul made a down payment of $400 which was 25% of the charge. What was the total charge? _____

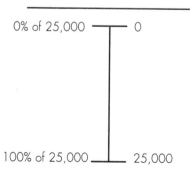

Last year, Ali earned $25,000. This year she should earn $30,000, which will be what percent of last year's income?

_____

0% of 25,000 ——— 0

100% of 25,000 ——— 25,000

PERCENT COMPUTATION

The word *percent* means "per cent" or "per hundred." The % sign therefore represents hundredths, which is the second decimal place. Many students rely solely on moving the decimal point two places to the right or to the left to convert decimals to percent or vice versa. Often, students move the decimal point without any thought to the numbers involved so that 0.5% becomes 50 instead of 0.005 or 0.9 becomes 9% instead of 90%. One initial activity has students identify the number of hundredths in a given number to determine the percent.

Example: How many hundredths are in each of the following numbers?

0.25	25 hundredths or 25%
0.8	80 hundredths or 80%
2.74	274 hundredths or 274%
0.005	0.5 hundredths or 0.5%

Since hundredths is the second decimal place, the % sign takes the place of two decimal places. Another activity involves counting the number of decimal places before and after the conversion.

Example: 85% contains two decimal places, so the 85 must be written in two places.   0.85
2% contains two decimal places, so the 2 must be written in two places.   0.02
0.5% contains three decimal places (0.5 has 1 + % has 2), so the 5 must be written in three places.   0.005
0.98 contains two decimal places, so it equals 98%.
0.5 contains one decimal place, so a "0" must be added. 0.50 equals 50%
0.042 contains three decimal places, since the % sign uses two of them, it equals 4.2%.

Whenever possible, emphasize the meaning and reasonableness of methods and answers.

PERCENTS AS PROPORTIONS

Activity: Students solve percent problems by first writing the related proportions.

Materials: activity sheet for each student

Comments: By definition, *percent* is the ratio "per hundred." As such, percent problems can be solved by writing a proportion with p/100 as one of the ratios. The equivalent ratio is the amount considered divided by the base quantity (the basis of the percent). Students often do not know "which number goes on top" or "which number goes on the bottom." They should be encouraged to consider which quantity is the basis of the comparison. That number is the base and is equivalent to 100%.

Two mnemonics are p/100 = a/b for amount/base and p/100 = is/of. As long as students understand the concept that the amount depends on the base, the mnemonics are useful. If not, then confusion as to "which number goes where" continues.

p/100 = is/of is useful for percent problems such as: "What is 60% of 72?" since the **is** quantity and **of** quantity are obvious. When a percent problem is given in context, the identification of the quantities may not be as obvious. For example, consider the problem:

> "Jill earned a commission of $3,000 on the $50,000 real estate transaction. What is the rate (percent) of commission?"

Three thousand dollars follows the word **of** but it is not the base quantity. Commissions are based on the amount of sales, which in this problem is the unknown. Students may be confused by the **is/of** mnemonic. It is important to discuss the amount (part) and on what that amount is based. Discuss the following:

amount of tax is based on amount of sales	p/100 = tax/sales amount
interest is based on the principal	p/100 = interest/principal
amount of discount is based on original cost	p/100 = discount/cost
amount of increase or decrease is based on the original amount*	p/100 = increase/original

* often the amount of increase or decrease has to be computed first.

PERCENTS AS PROPORTIONS

Solve the following problems by writing and solving a proportion: p/100 = amount/base

1. What is 80% of 40?

2. What is 12½% of 72?

3. 33 is 50% of what?

4. 60 is 200% of what number?

5. 75 is what % of 250?

6. 90 is what % of 30?

7. Ohio has a 5.5% sales tax. How much tax is owed on a $950 sofa?

8. Marty's money market paid Marty $30 in interest on a balance of $750. What is the interest rate on Marty's money market?

9. Joanne earns 6% commission on her sales. To earn $600, how much must Joanne sell?

10. The population increased from 27,400 to 28,300. What is the percent of increase in population (to the nearest percent)?

Percent Computation

PERCENTS AS EQUATIONS

Activity: Students will solve percent problems by translating the questions into equations.

Materials: activity sheet for each student

Comments: The translation of "amount is a percent of the base" is the equation model "amount = percent x base." The verb becomes the "equals" (the verb of the equation) and the "of" becomes multiplication. This model is very useful when the percent problem is in statement form. Some applied problems are easily translated when the student considers some common grammar rules, especially the antecedent of pronouns. For example:

Tom sold 28 newspapers, which is 70% of his goal. What is his goal?

"Which" refers back to the 28 newspapers, so the equation comes from "28 newspapers... is 70 % of what" or 28 = 70% x n.

Caution must be taken not to rely on "looking for the *of*" in an applied problem and assuming it precedes the base. For example:

Mr. Chen's investments earned an interest amount of $22.00. If the rate were 4.2%, how much was invested?

The *of* precedes $22.00. However, the $22.00 is the amount, not the base.
The correct equation is $22.00 = 4.2% x n—not n = 4.2% x $22.00.

PERCENTS AS EQUATIONS

Solve the following problems by writing and solving an equation.

1. What is 65% of 80?

2. 18 is 45% of what number?

3. 80 is what % of 200?

4. 15% of 80 is what number?

5. 30% of 90 is what number?

6. What % of 50 is 75?

7. Jamie bought a $150 coat on sale for 15% off. How much of a discount should she receive?

8. Ms. Tomis sold a $125,000 house and received a commission of $7,500. What was her rate of commission?

9. The Art Club raised $840, which was 70% of its goal. What was the club's goal?

10. Josh correctly answered 34 of the 40 test questions. If all the questions count the same, what percent should he receive?

LET'S BE DISCRETE I & II

Activity: Students are asked to determine the number of items in a set that corresponds to a given percent. "Let's Be Discrete I" has sets of 10 and 20 items, so each item represents 10% or 5%. "Let's Be Discrete II" has sets with various numbers of items.

Materials: activity sheet for each student

Comments: This activity can be adapted to various levels of instruction and student ability.

It can be used as an introductory activity. Students can write the percents as fractions, reduce to lowest terms, and circle the corresponding fractional amount.

For example: 75%   given 16 items
75%   becomes $^{75}/_{100}$ which reduces to ¾ so three out of every four is circled.

It could be used to reinforce or review the Proportion Model or the Equation Model of solving percent problems.

For example: 75%   given 16 items

Proportion Model $^{75}/_{100} = ^{n}/_{16}$
$$\frac{75 \times 16}{100} = \frac{100n}{100}$$
$$12 = n$$

Equation Model 75% of 16 = n
¾ × 16 = n
12 = n

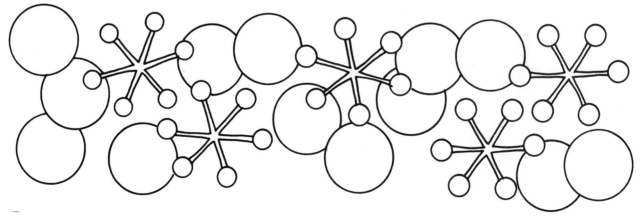

Let's Be Discrete I

Draw a circle around the given percent of each set of discrete items below.

1. 20%

2. 50%

3. 10%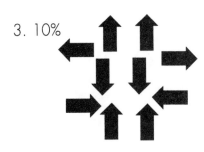

4. 70%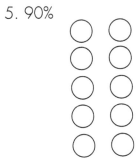

5. 90%

6. 80%

7. 15%

8. 60%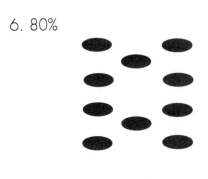

9. 40%

10. 35%

11. 45%

12. 25%.

LET'S BE DISCRETE II

Draw a circle around the given percent of each set of discrete items below.

1. 25%

2. 50%

3. 30%

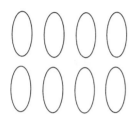

4. 75%

5. 20%

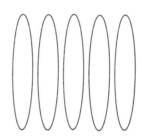

6. 80%

7. 15%

8. 48%

9. 40%

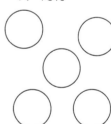

10. 64%

11. 90%

12. 24%

PERCENT MATCH

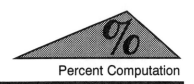
Activity: Students are asked to connect equivalent forms of fractions, decimals, and percent to answer a riddle.

Materials: activity sheet for each student

Comments: The activity includes the ⅛'s and ⅙'s equivalences. Therefore, it includes ½, ¼, and ⅓. The riddle refers to the Sieve of Eratosthenes, which could lead to a discussion reviewing prime and composite numbers.

PERCENT MATCH

Why was Eratosthenes such a lonely mathematician?

Connect the fraction from Column A to the equivalent decimal in Column B (use a ruler). Then connect that decimal to the equivalent percent in Column C. Place the letter from matching Column B to Column C above the corresponding number from matching Column A to Column B.

Column A	Column B	Column C
⅔ • ②	• 0.5 •	• 66⅔%
⅞ • ④ ⑤	• 0.6̄6 • Ⓔ Ⓐ	• 50%
½ •	• 0.875 •	• 37½%
⅓ •	• 0.375 • Ⓗ Ⓤ	• 87½%
¾ • ⑥ ①	• 0.75 • Ⓢ Ⓒ	• 25%
⅙ • ⑦	• 0.3̄3 •	• 83⅓%
⅜ • ③	• 0.25 • Ⓑ	• 75%
¼ • ⑧	• 0.833̄ • Ⓘ	• 33⅓%
⅝ • ⑪	• 0.125 • Ⓓ	• 16⅔%
⅚ •	• 0.16̄6 • Ⓝ	• 62½%
⅛ • ⑨ ⑩	• 0.625 • Ⓞ	• 12½%

___ ___ ___ ___ ___ ___ ___ ___ ___ ___ ___ ___ ___ ___ ___ ___
 1   2   3   4   5 6   2   7   2   7   4   8   9 10   10 9   2 11

Note: The Sieve of Eratosthenes is a chart and method for determining prime and composite numbers. Can you figure out the meaning of the riddle?

THREE-WAY MATCH

Activity: Students compare four items to determine the one that is not equivalent to the other three items. The letter associated with the nonequivalent form is written above the problem number in a riddle.

Materials: activity sheet for each student

Comments: This activity reviews several concepts involving percents, such as equivalent fractions and decimals, percent change, and commission, tax, and interest applications.

Since percent is a ratio, the amount (commission, tax, and interest) increases as the base amount (sales, cost, and principal) increases. In order for two amounts to stay equal, as the percent increases the base must decrease.

Example: 3% of $2,000 equals 6% of $ 1,000.
3 x ¹⁄₁₀₀ x 2,000 = 6 x ¹⁄₁₀₀ x 1,000 because
3 x ¹⁄₁₀₀ x 2 x 1,000 = 2 x 3 x ¹⁄₁₀₀ x 1,000   using
                 commutative and associative properties

This could lead to a discussion of direct and indirect variation.

 # THREE-WAY MATCH

In each set, determine which item does not belong. Write the corresponding letter above the problem number below.

1. ½ T   0.12 M   50% S   0.5 H

2. ¹⁵⁄₁₀₀ P   150% E   1.5 F   ¾ R

3. 0.625 A   62.5% V   62½% S   6.25 N

4. ⅔ K   2.3 E   66⅔% T   .6̄6̄6̄ N

5. 2¼% H   0.0225 A   2.25 I   2.25% W

6. 60% of 20 W   20% of 60 H   10% of 30 V   10% of 120 T

7. 30% of 40 E   15% of 20 R   60% of 20 S   15% of 80 C

8. 15% of 10 O   150% of 100 E   100% of 150 T ⅔ of 100 H

9. ½% of 20 L   5% of 20 G   0.5% of 20 K   20% of 0.5 D

10. 8% of 10 E   ⅒ of 80 F   20% of 40 G   10% of 80 H

11. percent change   percent change   percent change   percent change
    from 20 to 30 N   from 60 to 90 S   from 25 to 50 E   from 40 to 60 Y

12. percent change   percent change   percent change   percent change
    from 30 to 20 A   from 15 to 10 B   from 60 to 30 C   from 36 to 24 D

13. $100 at 4% for $100 at 1% for $100 at 2% for $100 at 8% for
    2 years   M   4 years   N   4 years   W   1 year   V

14. 3% tax on $6.00 E   6% tax on $12.00 F   4% tax on $18.00 G   8% tax on $9.00 H

15. 2% commission on   4% commission on   6% commission on   5% commission on
    sales of $20,000 D   sales of $10,000 N   sales of $60,000 X   sales of $8,000 I

16. 20% discount on a   10% discount on a   25% discount on a   15% discount on a
    $25 jacket   U $50 jacket   O $20 jacket   E $60 jacket   I

"Changing decimals to percents and percents to decimals is a

___ ___ ___ ___ ___ ___   ___ ___ ___ ___ ___ ___ ___ ___ ___ ___ ___ "
1   8   6   5   13 9   10 15 2   4   7   16 11 3   12 14

GET THE POINT?

Activity: For problems #1-16, students estimate answers to percent problems given multiple choices. For problems #17-20, students locate the decimal point of an answer, given the digits of the answer.

Materials: activity sheet for each student

Comments: Prior to this activity, discuss reference percents, such as 10%, 25%, 50%, and 75%, and comparing the amount to the base:

10% of a quantity can be found by moving the decimal point one place.
25% is ¼ of a quantity, less than half
50% is ½ of a quantity
75% is ¾ of a quantity, more than half

An amount approximately equal to the base results in a percent close to 100%.
An amount approximately equal to about ½ the base results in a percent close to 50%.
An amount approximately equal to about ¼ of the base results in a percent close to 25%.
An amount greater than the base results in a percent greater than 100%.

Often it is easier to eliminate unreasonable answers to determine the correct answer.

GET THE POINT?

Choose the best estimate for each problem. Do NOT compute exact answers.

1. 34% of 427 is about   A. 0.15   B. 1.5   C. 15   D. 150

2. 22% of 55 is about   A. 0.12   B. 1.2   C. 12   D. 120

3. 75% of 39 is about   A. 0.3   B. 3   C. 30   D. 300

4. 95% of 181 is about   A. 0.17   B. 1.7   C. 17   D. 170

5. 0.5% of 84 is about   A. 0.4   B. 4   C. 40   D. 400

6. 0.2% of 5 is about   A. 0.01   B. 0.1   C. 1   D. 10

7. 125% of 30 is about   A. 0.45   B. 4.5   C. 45   D. 450

8. 200% of 610 is about   A. 1.2   B. 12   C. 120   D. 1200

9. 15 out of 48 is about   A. 0.3%   B. 3%   C. 30%   D. 300%

10. 56 out of 60 is about   A. 0.9%   B. 9%   C. 90%   D. 900%

11. 2 compared to 320 is about   A. 0.6%   B. 6%   C. 16%   D. 160%

12. 625 compared to 420 is about   A. 66%   B. 660%   C. 15%   D. 150%

13. 50 is 60% of about   A. 3   B. 30   C. 80   D. 800

14. 50 is 120% of about   A. 40   B. 400   C. 6   D. 60

15. 7 is 34% of about   A. 50   B. 5   C. 20   D. 200

16. 7 is 140% of about   A. 50   B. 5   C. 20   D. 200

Place a decimal point to make a true statement (insert 0's if needed).

17. 80% of 2,000 is   1 6 0 0 0

18. 0.5% of 900 is   4 5 0 0

19. 70 out of 800 is   0 8 7 5 %

20. 60 is 30% of   0 2 0 0

Activity: Students calculate percents by using ten percent and one percent as reference percents. Ten percent is found by moving the decimal point one place to the left. One percent is found by moving the decimal point two places to the left. The desired percent is found by multiplying the results by the appropriate factor.

Materials: activity sheet for each student

Comments: The activity sheet presents step-by-step directions on the procedure. Additional problems could be modeled on the overhead or board. Additional problems could be assigned.

A PERFECT TEN PERCENT

Ten percent of a quantity is easy to calculate since 10% equals ¹⁄₁₀, which is the same as dividing by 10 or moving the decimal point one place to the left. By multiplying the amount by 2, 3, or ½, you can find 20%, 30%, or 5% of an amount.

Examples: Find 30% of 130.   10% of 130 is 13 so 30% (or 3 x 10%) is 3 x 13 or 39
            Find 5% of 130.   10% of 130 is 13 so 5% (or ½ x 10%) is ½ x 13 or 6.5
            Find 35% of 130.   35% is the same as 30% + 5% or 39 + 6.5 = 45.5

Use 10% to find the following:

1. 20% of 420   10% of 420 is _____ so 20% (or _____ x 10%) is _____ x _____ = _____

2. 5% of 420   10% of 420 is _____ so 5% (or _____ x 10%) is _____ x _____ = _____

3. 25% of 420   25% is 20% + 5% or _____ + _____ = _____

4. 80% of 70   10% of 70 is _____ so 80% (or _____ x 10%) is _____ x _____ = _____

5. 5% of 70   10% of 70 is _____ so 5% (or _____ x 10%) is _____ x _____ = _____

6. 85% of 70   85% is 80% + 5% or _____ + _____ = _____

One percent of a quantity is also easy to calculate since 1% equals ¹⁄₁₀₀, which is the same as dividing by 100 or moving the decimal point two places to the left.

Example: Find 3% of 420.   1% of 420 is 4.2 so 3% (or 3 x 1%) is 3 x 4.2 or 12.6

Use 1% to find the following:

7. 6% of 110   1% of 110 is _____ so 6% (or _____ x 1%) is _____ x _____ = _____

8. 4% of 900   1% of 900 is _____ so 4% (or _____ x 1%) is_____ x _____ = _____

Use 10% and 1% to find the following:

9. 77% of 120   10% of 120 is _____ so 70% is _____.
            1% of 120 is _____ so 7% is _____. Therefore, 77% is _____.

10. 88% of 400   10% of 400 is _____ so 80% is _____.
            1% of 400 is _____ so 8% is _____. Therefore, 88% is _____.

PERCENT AND COMMON SENSE

Common sense is a relative term. It depends on students' experiences. What "makes sense" to one person may or may not "make sense" to another. Activities throughout this book provide experiences with percent concepts through percent models and percent computation.

This section provides opportunities for teachers to discuss reasonableness of percent quantities. Special emphasis should be given to deciding when percents greater than 100% are appropriate. Whereas, costs can increase by more than 100%, they cannot decrease by more than 100%. For example, a coat could be purchased for $50 and then sold for $60 (120% of the $50). A coat purchased for $50 would not be sold for –$10 (decrease of 120%).

Another topic for additional emphasis is deciding when events are mutually exclusive. A person cannot be in two different classes at the same time. Yet someone could order more than one item for lunch. Surveys involving "a favorite item" imply mutually exclusive responses and the results should total 100%. Surveys asking for "use or preference" allow for more than one response. Each item mentioned could have 100% respondents. Such a survey often results in totals greater than 100%.

"A Potpourri of Percent Problems" offers some interesting percent tidbits and suggests additional discussion opportunities. Teachers are encouraged to make students aware of the use of percent, have them contact companies concerning consumer claims involving percent, and to question results.

ALL "ABOUT" PERCENT

Activity: Students are asked to complete statements using estimated percents: 0%, about 10%, about 25%, about 50%, about 75%, about 90%, and 100%.

Materials: one activity sheet for each student

Comments: This activity lends itself to discussing percent in terms of comparing the specified amount (for example, students who are right-handed) to the base of reference (students in the class). The number of students satisfying a given condition does not give the percent. The number must be compared to the base population. As an example, 22 out of 25 students being right-handed results in an answer of "about 90%." But, 22 out of 250 students in the school being absent results in an answer of "about 10%." This type of discussion reinforces the concept of percent as a ratio with a comparative base of 100.

Students might be asked how they could check the accuracy of their estimates. Items #12 and #13 do not lend themselves to a survey or counting activity by students. Weather agencies, however, do base their percents on the number of times in the past that the given weather conditions have resulted in certain forms of precipitation and temperature readings.

Discuss what *0% chance* and *100% chance* mean.

ALL "ABOUT" PERCENT

Choose the best percent estimate for each of the following statements.

Estimates: A. 0%
            B. About 10%
            C. About 25%
            D. About 50%
            E. About 75%
            F. About 90%
            G. 100%

Statement:

1. _____ of the students in my class are girls.
2. _____ of the students in my class have a pet.
3. _____ of the students in my class are right-handed.
4. _____ of the students in my class are 7 feet tall.
5. _____ of the students in my class are wearing athletic shoes.
6. _____ of the students in my school were absent yesterday.
7. _____ of the students in my school brought their lunch today.
8. _____ of the faculty and staff of my school are male.
9. _____ of the cars in the parking lot are red.
10. _____ of the school buses are yellow.
11. _____ of the parking spaces are taken.
12. _____ chance of snow today.
13. _____ chance that the temperature outdoors will be greater than 50 degrees.

Complete the following:

14. 0% of _____.

15. 100% of _____.

Activity: Students are asked to decide the reasonableness of statements containing percents less than and greater than 100%.

Materials: one activity sheet for each student
optional: transparency of activity sheet for discussion

Comments: Some statements (#1, #14, and #15) depend on whether the categories are mutually exclusive. For instance, in #1, a person *may* have ordered a hot dog *and* French fries. Whereas, in #15, a student would *not* have math and P.E. the same period.

Some statements involve percents greater than 100%. For #10, a stock *may* *increase* by more than 100%, but it *cannot decrease* by more than 100%. If it could, what would that mean? Would the stockbroker have to *pay you* to buy the stock?

This activity lends itself to class discussion and journal or math log entries. Some suggestions include:

Explain why the nonsense statements are not reasonable.
Rewrite the nonsense statements so they make sense.
What is a reasonable APR for a car loan?
How many problems were on the quiz in #3?
How many questions were on the test in #4?
What would be a reasonable sales tax for an $8.00 purchase?
What is the equivalent percent reduction for 50% off with an additional
      50% off? Suggest using an original price of $100.
What is Sean's average?

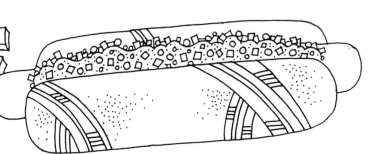

Common Sense: Sense or Nonsense %

Decide whether each statement is reasonable.

Use an S for sense and an N for nonsense.

1. ____ When the Ames family went out to eat, 50% of them ordered hamburgers, 50% ordered hot dogs, 50% ordered French fries, and 50% ordered juice.

2. ____ The bank charges an annual percentage rate of 75% for a car loan.

3. ____ Shannon missed three problems on a quiz and scored a 75%.

4. ____ Jamie missed four questions on a test and scored 80%.

5. ____ The Lincoln High Lions won 120% of their games.

6. ____ Ali paid $4.00 sales tax for an $8.00 purchase.

7. ____ Price of gasoline has increased more than 200% since 1972.

8. ____ A 50% chance of rain on Saturday and a 50% chance of rain on Sunday means there is a 100% chance of rain during the weekend.

9. ____ A sale item marked 50% off with an additional 50% off is free.

10. ____ The stock value decreased 110%.

11. ____ Sean averaged his grades of 77%, 72%, 81%, and 73% to be 80%.

12. ____ Al was so hungry, he ate 125% of the cake.

13. ____ Ahmad correctly answered 45 of 50 questions and received a grade of 90%.

14. ____ The class survey showed that 75% of the class liked football, 50% liked basketball, but only 25% liked baseball.

15. ____ The class survey showed that 30% of the class had math second period, 40% had P.E. second period, and 40% had English second period.

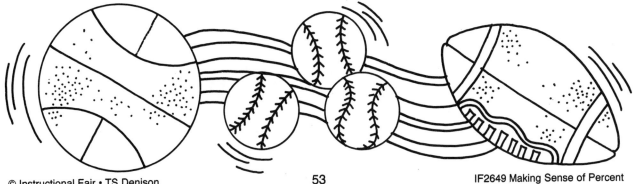

LET'S BE REASONABLE

Activity: Students determine the reasonableness of the answers given to percent applications. If the answer is incorrect, students explain why and determine the correct answer. Hopefully, the activity and associated discussion will uncover and address percent misconceptions.

Materials: one activity sheet for each student
optional: transparency of the activity sheet for class discussion

Comments: Some of the mathematics concepts highlighted in this activity include the commutativity of multiplication, addition and subtraction of percents, percent as a ratio based on 100, and equivalent percents and decimals. A discussion before the activity might include:

Is the cost of an item 50% off, with an additional 25% off, the same as the item with 75% off?

> No, for example, an $80 coat with 50% off is $40 and with an additional 25% off is $30. The same coat with 75% off is $20. The 50% off is based on the original price ($80), whereas the 25% off is based on the first sale price ($60). Fifty percent of $80 cannot be added to 25% of $60.

Is the cost of an item 25% off with an additional 50% off the same as 50% off with an additional 25% off?

> Yes. For example, using the same $80 coat, with 25% off ($60) with an additional 50% off is $30. This is the same amount as above. This result might surprise several students.

> Another approach is to consider the *amount paid* as opposed to the *amount off*. Twenty-five percent means you pay 75%. So the question becomes "Is 50% of 75% of an amount the same as 75% of 50% of an amount?" Translated it becomes: "Is $0.5 \times 0.75 \times n$ equal to $0.75 \times 0.5 \times n$?" Since multiplication is commutative, the answer is yes.

Is it true that the larger the percent, the larger the quantity?

> No, 2% of 1,000 or 20 is greater than 20% of 40 or 8.

The wholesale price of a $200 coat was increased by 20% for retail. It was then put on sale 20% off. Is the sale price $200?

> No, $200 + 20% = $200 + $40 = $240.
> Whereas, $240 - 20% = $240 - $48 = $192.

LET'S BE REASONABLE

Decide whether each situation is reasonable. If not, state the error that is made. Correct the situation.

1. A $90.00 watch on sale for 30% off is marked $60.00.

2. Mark can buy a $100 bicycle on sale at 20% off. If he pays cash, he receives an additional 5% off. Mark figures he will pay $75.00 in cash for the bike.

3. Jo can buy two $50 skirts on sale for 25% off or she can take advantage of the "Buy One, Get One ½ Off" special. Jo figures the money saved is the same.

4. Ali can open a $1,000 CD account for 3 months at a rate of 6% followed by 9 months at a rate of 5%. Another bank has a 12-month $1,000 CD for 5.5%. Ali figures the interest will be the same since the average of 5% and 6% is 5.5%.

5. The news report states that the cost for a gallon of gasoline was 110% of last year's price. Mary said that it could not be correct since 100% is the total price. Anne said she thought the report could be right.

6. The club membership went from 75 to 90 members and then dropped down to 75. Tom mentioned that the percent of decrease was the same as the percent of increase.

The following are some interesting situations, problems, and improbable percents.

Ivory Soap: 99⁴⁴/₁₀₀% pure—it floats

Believe it or not, the above statement is based on fact and is not just an advertising slogan. According to Procter & Gamble Consumer Relations Department, in the 1800s, samples of Ivory were sent for analysis. The comparison was made with castile soap—the standard at the time. One chemist's analysis was in table form with the ingredients listed by percentages. Harley Procter totaled the ingredients which did not fall into the category of pure soap—they equaled ⁵⁶/₁₀₀. He subtracted from 100 and wrote the slogan, "99⁴⁴/₁₀₀% Pure."

Students should be encouraged to research consumer claims. Several products have addresses or (800) phone numbers listed on the labels. Students could write to the Public Relations Departments of the companies requesting information concerning the claims.

When does a 98%-accurate test result in a 20% test result?

This is one of several seemingly improbable statistics included in *Innumeracy* by John Paulos. Most people think a 98%-accurate test implies that a positive test result means a 98% chance of having a disease or whatever is being tested. The example demonstrates the effect of even the smallest of percents when the base is a very large number. A similar example follows: Assume that six out of every 1,000 people have a certain disease. Then roughly 600 people of a 100,000-population city would have the disease. A 98%-accurate test is developed. The population of 100,000 are given the test. 98% of the 600 (or 588) with the disease should test positive. Two percent of the disease-free 99,400 people (or 1988) will also test positive. Of the total positive tests (588 + 1,988 = 2,576), most are false positives. Therefore, someone testing positive has a 588 out of 2576 chance (or 22.8%) of being a true positive.

This example demonstrates how a small percent of a very large number can compare with a large percent of a small number.

The following question was posed at a national math competition and appeared in the *Knoxville News-Sentinel*, April, 1995.

"Out of 200 fish in an aquarium, 99% are guppies. How many guppies must be removed so that the percent of guppies in the aquarium is 98%?"

A common first response is 2 guppies since there is a change of 1% and 1% of 200 is 2. However, 98% of 200 is 198. There are 198 guppies and 2 other fish. The 2 other fish become 2% of the remaining fish after the guppies are removed. Two is 2% of 100, so only 98 guppies can remain. One hundred guppies must be removed.

PERCENT GAMES

Games can be used to reinforce concepts already studied. This section includes suggestions for file folder games that can be used in activity sheet format and card games. The percent concepts include equating shaded areas to percents; calculating fraction and percent equivalences with or without a calculator; comparing percent quantities; calculating interest; and solving percent proportions.

It must be noted that calculators are "not created equal," especially concerning percent. If students are using a variety of calculators in the classroom, additional instruction may be needed for some of the game rules. When the % key is used, some calculators will show the decimal equivalent in the display. Other calculators do not show the change in decimal point location. The order in which a problem is keyed in also varies from one calculator to another. For example, to calculate 25% of 40 may require keying in 25% x 40 = or 40 x 25%. Some calculators will show amount of the percent and then the quantity amount in one statement. For example, for the situation of a $60 coat at 20% off, some calculators allow the student to input 60 – 20% and will show 12 (the discount) in the display and then after the = is pressed will show 48 (the sale price).

NAME THAT PERCENT SPIN

To make a file folder game, write the title on the folder tab. Cut out and glue the instructions on the front of the folder. Cut out and glue the chart of percents on the inside left side and the circle of shapes on the inside right side. Students can use a pencil and paper clip as a spinner. Put the pencil point through the end of the paper clip and on the center of the circle of shapes. Use the paper clip as a pointer.

Instructions:

Topic: Identify equivalent percents given fractional shapes
            Strategic game playing

Players: 2-4

Material: Gameboard
            20 counters for each player (different color for each player)

Object: Have the highest score

Rules: 1. The first player spins and gives the equivalent percent for the shaded shape.
            2. The player then finds the squares with that percent on the chart and places one counter to score the greatest number of points.
            3. If the player does not know the percent, gives an incorrect percent, or cannot play on the board, he/she loses a turn.
            4. The next player then does steps 1-3.
            5. The game continues until one person plays all of his or her counters, or the gameboard is completely covered.

Scoring: 3 points for 3 counters in a row
            5 points for 4 counters in a row
            10 points for 5 counters in a row
            15 points for 6 counters in a row
            20 points for 7 counters in a row

NAME THAT PERCENT SPIN

40%	30%	60%	20%	80%	10%	66⅔%
50%	75%	12½%	70%	40%	37½%	62½%
66⅔%	10%	30%	25%	33⅓%	62½%	25%
60%	33⅓%	37½%	50%	40%	75%	20%
90%	62½%	50%	90%	37½%	12½%	75%
80%	12½%	70%	33⅓%	90%	50%	70%
25%	30%	20%	10%	60%	80%	66⅔%

NAME THAT PERCENT SPIN

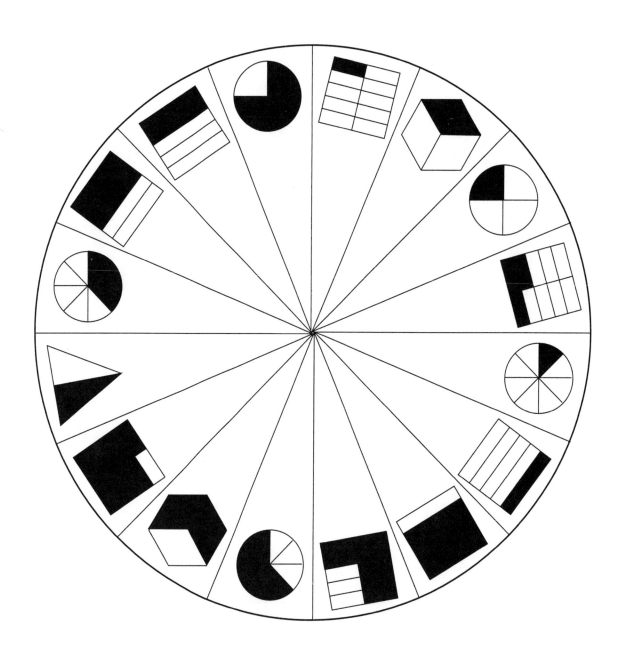

I Have. Who Has? Circle Game

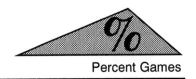

Activity: Students identify fraction, decimal, and percent equivalences.

Materials: A deck of I HAVE. WHO HAS? cards—enough cards for each student to have one.

Procedure: Construction:

Make a list of the equivalences you want to use.   EX. $\frac{1}{4} = 25\%$
(List at least one equivalence for each student.) $\frac{2}{3} = 66\frac{2}{3}\%$
Do not repeat. For instance, do not use $\frac{1}{8} = 12\frac{1}{2}\%$
$\frac{1}{4} = 25\%$ and $0.25 = 25\%$ $\frac{1}{3} = 33\frac{1}{3}\%$
                                                          $\frac{5}{8} = 62\frac{1}{2}\%$

Take a deck of blank cards (index cards work well). On one side, print *I Have.* On the other side, print *Who Has.* Take the first card. Write the first fraction ($\frac{1}{4}$) on the *I Have* side, and the second percent ($66\frac{2}{3}\%$) on the *Who Has* side.

Take the next card, and write the second fraction ($\frac{2}{3}$) on the *I Have* side and the third percent ($12\frac{1}{2}\%$) on the *Who Has* side. Continue.

On the last card, write the last fraction ($\frac{5}{8}$) on the *I Have* side, and the first percent (25%) on the *Who Has* side. You have completed the circle.

Distribute the cards—one per student. Extras can be played by the teacher or given out to students. Choose any student to start. The first student reads the *Who Has* side. The student with the equivalent *I Have* card reads it and the *Who Has* side. Continue. The last person's *Who Has* side should be the first person's *I Have.*

To keep the attention of students who have read their cards, have them list the equivalences as they are read. It not only keeps their attention, but it serves as a review of the information. Sample lists are provided. The activity can be adapted to other concepts involving equivalences or definitions.

Common fractions and percents:

1. $\frac{1}{2} = 50\%$
2. $\frac{1}{3} = 33\frac{1}{3}\%$
3. $\frac{2}{3} = 66\frac{2}{3}\%$
4. $\frac{1}{4} = 25\%$
5. $\frac{3}{4} = 75\%$
6. $\frac{1}{5} = 20\%$
7. $\frac{2}{5} = 40\%$
8. $\frac{3}{5} = 60\%$
9. $\frac{4}{5} = 80\%$
10. $\frac{1}{6} = 16\frac{2}{3}\%$
11. $\frac{5}{6} = 83\frac{1}{3}\%$
12. $\frac{1}{8} = 12\frac{1}{2}\%$
13. $\frac{3}{8} = 37\frac{1}{2}\%$
14. $\frac{5}{8} = 62\frac{1}{2}\%$
15. $\frac{7}{8} = 87\frac{1}{2}\%$
16. $\frac{1}{10} = 10\%$
17. $\frac{3}{10} = 30\%$
18. $\frac{7}{10} = 70\%$
19. $\frac{9}{10} = 90\%$
20. $\frac{1}{20} = 5\%$
21. $\frac{3}{20} = 15\%$
22. $\frac{7}{20} = 35\%$
23. $\frac{9}{20} = 45\%$
24. $\frac{11}{20} = 55\%$
25. $\frac{13}{20} = 65\%$
26. $\frac{17}{20} = 85\%$
27. $\frac{19}{20} = 95\%$
28. $\frac{1}{1} = 100\%$
29. $\frac{3}{2} = 150\%$
30. $\frac{2}{1} = 200\%$

Fractions and percents for calculator practice:

1. $\frac{1}{12} = 8\frac{1}{3}\%$
2. $\frac{5}{12} = 41\frac{2}{3}\%$
3. $\frac{7}{12} = 58\frac{1}{3}\%$
4. $\frac{11}{12} = 91\frac{2}{3}\%$
5. $\frac{1}{15} = 6\frac{2}{3}\%$
6. $\frac{2}{15} = 13\frac{1}{3}\%$
7. $\frac{4}{15} = 26\frac{2}{3}\%$
8. $\frac{7}{15} = 46\frac{2}{3}\%$
9. $\frac{8}{15} = 53\frac{1}{3}\%$
10. $\frac{11}{15} = 73\frac{1}{3}\%$
11. $\frac{13}{15} = 86\frac{2}{3}\%$
12. $\frac{14}{15} = 93\frac{1}{3}\%$
13. $\frac{1}{9} = 11\frac{1}{9}\%$
14. $\frac{2}{9} = 22\frac{2}{9}\%$
15. $\frac{4}{9} = 44\frac{4}{9}\%$
16. $\frac{5}{9} = 55\frac{5}{9}\%$
17. $\frac{7}{9} = 77\frac{7}{9}\%$
18. $\frac{8}{9} = 88\frac{8}{9}\%$
19. $\frac{1}{11} = 9\frac{1}{11}\%$
20. $\frac{2}{11} = 18\frac{2}{11}\%$
21. $\frac{3}{11} = 27\frac{3}{11}\%$
22. $\frac{4}{11} = 36\frac{4}{11}\%$
23. $\frac{5}{11} = 45\frac{5}{11}\%$
24. $\frac{6}{11} = 54\frac{6}{11}\%$
25. $\frac{7}{11} = 63\frac{7}{11}\%$
26. $\frac{8}{11} = 72\frac{8}{11}\%$
27. $\frac{9}{11} = 81\frac{9}{11}\%$
28. $\frac{10}{11} = 90\frac{10}{11}\%$

PERCENT RUMMY

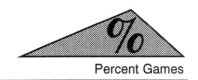

Activity: Students play a form of rummy, making sets of equivalent fractions, decimals, and percents.

Materials: a deck of Percent Rummy cards for each small group of students

Procedure: The decks of cards can be made ahead of time, or they can be made by students as a review activity.

Make a list of 17 to 20 fraction, decimal, and percent equivalences. Write one of each on the top half of a blank card. (Index cards work well.) Seventeen to 20 sets make decks of 51 to 60 cards each.

Players: 2–4

Object: To play all the cards in your hand.
If more than one game is played,
the player with the most points win.

Rules: Six cards are dealt to each player for three or four players; nine cards each are dealt for two players. The remaining cards are placed face down in the middle (the stock).
The top card is turned over and placed next to the stock and forms the discard pile.
The player to the left of the dealer draws one card from the stock or the discard pile.
If the player has three of a kind (equivalent fraction, decimal, percent), he/she places them face up on the table. If the three are not equivalent, the player must place them back in his/her hand.
When the player has played all cards possible, the player discards one card.
The next player can either take the top card from the stock or the discard pile. Play continues.
The game is over when a player has played all of his/her cards. That player is the winner of the game.
If more than one game is played, when a player plays all of his/her cards, the other players count the cards they still have in their hands and give that number of points to the winner.
The champion is the player with the most points at the end of all games.

Activity: Students play a form of "Go Fish" to review equivalent fractions, decimals, and percents.

Materials: a deck of Percent Hunt cards for each small group

Procedure: The decks of cards can be made ahead of time, or they can be made by students as a review activity.

Make a list of 25 pairs of equivalences—equivalent fraction and percent and equivalent decimal and percent. Write one of each pair on the top half of a blank card. (Index cards work well.) Twenty-five pairs make a deck of 50 cards.

Players: 2-4

Object: To play all the cards in your hand.

Rules: Five cards are dealt to each player.
The remaining cards are placed face down in the middle (the stack).
The player to the left of the dealer asks any other player if he has a card equal to some card in the player's hand. (If he has a ¾ card, he may ask for the 75%. If he has a 75% card, he may ask for a card equal to 75%.)
If the asked player has the card requested, he gives it to the first player. The pair of cards (one of which must be a %) is placed face up on the table.
The player gets another turn.
If the asked player does not have the requested card, he says "Percent Hunt."
The first player then draws a card from the stack.
If he draws the requested card, he plays again.
If he does not draw the requested card, the new card is placed in his hand and his turn is finished.
The next player takes his turn.
Play continues until one player runs out of cards.
That player is the winner.

PERCENT TOURNAMENT

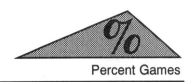

Activity: Students in pairs or small groups use the product and the sum of two digits to make a fraction. The fraction is converted to its equivalent percent. The percents are compared in a tournament fashion to determine the Percent Tournament Champion.

Materials: activity sheet for each student
two numbered spinners (or two dice) for each pair or small group of students

Procedure: Each student spins the two spinners. The student finds the product and sum of the two numbers. The fraction formed by dividing the product by the sum is then changed to a percent rounded to the nearest tenth. Students check one another's results. The percents are compared in pairs like rounds in a tournament. The greater percent is the winner of each round. Each student determines his/her Champion. The students in each group compare their results to determine the Group Tournament Champion.

Example: Spin a 2 and 3. The product is 6 and the sum is 5. The fraction % becomes 120%. Compare this percent with the other percent in the same round to determine the greater percent. After the eighth round, students compare their final results.

Variations: The fraction could be formed by dividing the sum by the product. If the spinners have a zero space, the player spinning a zero would not be able to calculate a percent (division by zero is undefined).

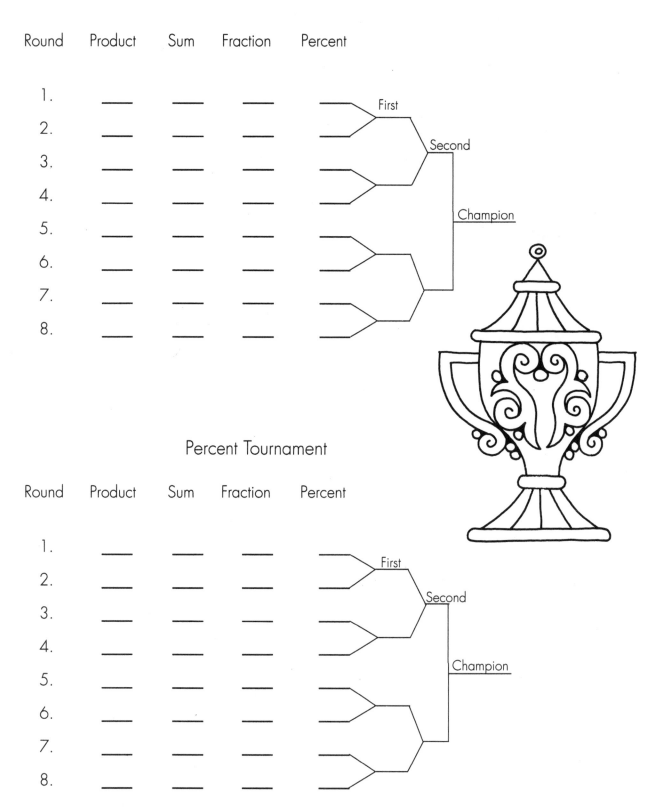

Round	Product	Sum	Fraction	Percent
1.	___	___	___	___
2.	___	___	___	___
3.	___	___	___	___
4.	___	___	___	___
5.	___	___	___	___
6.	___	___	___	___
7.	___	___	___	___
8.	___	___	___	___

First

Second

Champion

Percent Tournament

Round	Product	Sum	Fraction	Percent
1.	___	___	___	___
2.	___	___	___	___
3.	___	___	___	___
4.	___	___	___	___
5.	___	___	___	___
6.	___	___	___	___
7.	___	___	___	___
8.	___	___	___	___

First

Second

Champion

An "Interest"ing Game

Activity: The activity is a game played by pairs or small groups. Students calculate interest amounts and resulting balances using various interest rates—5%, 10%, 15%, and 20%. The activity lends itself to calculator use.

Materials: activity sheet for each pair or group of students
pencil and paper clip to use with spinners
calculator for each group

Comments: Discuss when interest is paid and when it is received. Discuss reasonable interest rates such as 5% for money market accounts, 10% for car loans, 15% for some investment possibilities, 20% for credit card balances.

Some calculators will calculate the interest and balance in "one statement."
Example: 15% and Receive with a starting balance of $100.00
Keystrokes: 100 + 15% =
After using the % and before hitting the = , the display will show the amount of interest.

 # An "Interest"ing Game

Interest is the amount of money charged for borrowed money. You pay interest when you borrow money (take out a loan) and you receive interest when you lend money. In this game, you will calculate the interest for various amounts at various rates of interest.

Playing the Game:

1) Each player makes a chart: <u>Rate</u>   <u>Interest</u>   <u>Pay</u>   <u>Receive</u>   <u>Balance</u>
                                                                                                $100.00

First Player:

2) Spin the Percent Spinner to find the interest rate. Calculate the amount of interest.

3) Spin the Pay/Receive Spinner. If Pay, subtract the interest from the balance. If Receive, add the interest to the balance.

Second (and remaining) Player(s):

4) Repeat steps 2 and 3.

5) The first player to reach $150.00 wins. Any player reaching $0.00 is out of the game.

Example (After two rounds with two players):

First player:	Rate	Interest	Pay	Receive	Balance
					$100.00
1st spin: 10% and Pay	10% x $100.00 =	$10.00	-$10.00		$ 90.00
2nd spin: 15% and Receive	15% x $ 90.00 =	$13.50		+$13.50	$103.50

Second player:	Rate	Interest	Pay	Receive	Balance
					$100.00
1st spin: 20% and Receive	20% x $100.00 =	$20.00		+$20.00	$120.00
2nd spin: 5% and Pay	5% x $120.00 =	$6.00	-$6.00		$114.00

Percent Spinner   **Pay/Receive Spinner**

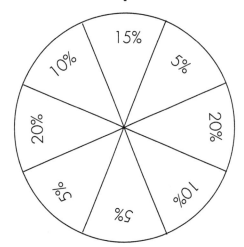

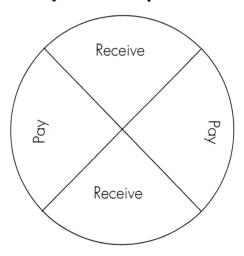

Percent Trail

To make a file folder game, write the title on the the folder tab. Cut out and glue the instructions on the front of the folder. Cut out the two path sections. Glue the *Start* half on the inside left side of the folder. Glue the *Finish* half on the inside right side, making certain that the two sections are aligned at the center of the folder. Avoid gluing across the fold of the folder.

Instructions:

Topic: Determine the missing part of a percent proportion.

Players: 2-4

Material: gameboard
            cube or spinner
            playing piece or counter for each player

Object: To reach Finish first.

Rules: 1. First player rolls the cube or spins the spinner and moves the appropriate number
               of spaces.

            2. The player then states the missing quantity in the percent proportion.

            3. If the player cannot furnish the correct answer, the playing piece is returned to the
               previous space.

            4. The next player then does step 1.

            5. Game continues until one player reaches Finish.

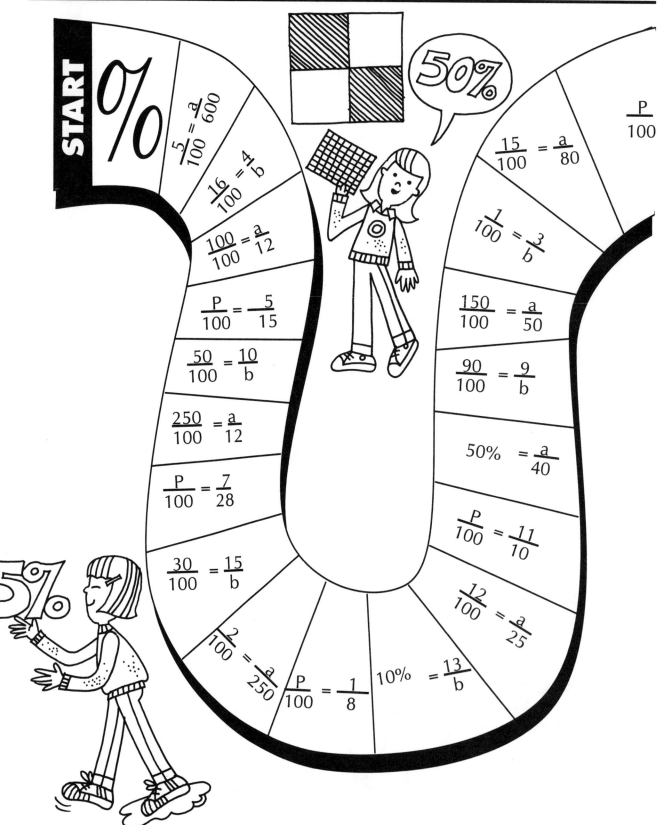

START %

$\dfrac{5}{100} = \dfrac{a}{600}$

$\dfrac{16}{100} = \dfrac{4}{b}$

$\dfrac{100}{100} = \dfrac{a}{12}$

$\dfrac{P}{100} = \dfrac{5}{15}$

$\dfrac{50}{100} = \dfrac{10}{b}$

$\dfrac{250}{100} = \dfrac{a}{12}$

$\dfrac{P}{100} = \dfrac{7}{28}$

$\dfrac{30}{100} = \dfrac{15}{b}$

$\dfrac{2}{100} = \dfrac{a}{250}$

$\dfrac{P}{100} = \dfrac{1}{8}$

10% $= \dfrac{13}{b}$

50%

$\dfrac{15}{100} = \dfrac{a}{80}$

$\dfrac{1}{100} = \dfrac{3}{b}$

$\dfrac{150}{100} = \dfrac{a}{50}$

$\dfrac{90}{100} = \dfrac{9}{b}$

50% $= \dfrac{a}{40}$

$\dfrac{P}{100} = \dfrac{11}{10}$

$\dfrac{12}{100} = \dfrac{a}{25}$

$\dfrac{P}{100}$

5%

Trail

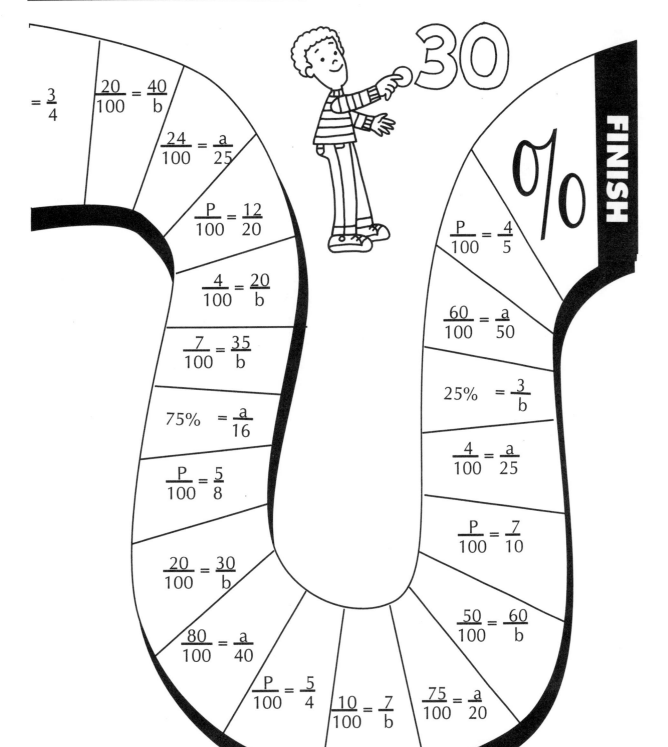

Percent Games

Percent Square

Activity: Students work in small groups to match equivalent percent, decimal, and fraction quantities to form a square.

Materials: Percent Square puzzle pieces for each small group

Comments: Make several copies of the puzzle below, cut the small squares apart, and place them in small bags or envelopes. Give one bag or envelope to each small group.

Percent Square Puzzle Pieces

0.03 / 60% of 30	3% / 50%	75% of 40 ; 30 / 20%	10% of 10 ; 1 / 25%
18 ; 80% of 100 / ¾%	0.5 ; 80 / 10	½% ; 3⁄10 ; 30% / 0.05	¼ ; 20% of 60 ; 12 / ¾
0.0075 ; 3⁄20 / 90%	5% of 200 ; 15% ; 0.009 / 25	5% ; 0.9% ; 0.1% / 2.5	75% ; 0.001 / 150%
½% ; 3⁄5 / 60%	50% of 50 ; 60% / 5	250% ; 25% of 20 / 5	1.5 ; 0.1 / 10%

Answer Key

Shady Percents
Page 3

1. 50	2. 40
3. 25	4. 36
5. 64	6. 9
7. 12	8. 28-30
9. 10-12	

Estimating Percents I
Page 5

1. 75%	2. 25%
3. 50%	4. 100%
5. 50%	6. 75%
7. 1%	8. 150%
9. 25%	10. 100%

Estimating Percents II
Page 6

1. 50%	2. 25%
3. 1%	4. 50%
5. 75%	

6. 40%   7. 20%   8. 90%   9. 10%   10. 70%

     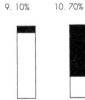

Number Chart Percent
Page 8

1. 50	2. 20
3. 10	4. 10
5. 25	6. 74
7. 19	8. 24
9. 30	10. 45 or 46*

*depends on whether 100 is included

Shady Pictures I
Page 10

1. 23%   2. 15½%

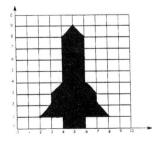 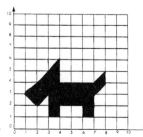

Shady Pictures II
Page 11

1. 30%   2. 19%

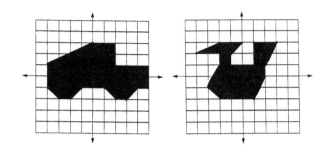

What's the Percent? I
Page 13

1. 8 out of 10	80%
2. 3 out of 10	30%
3. 7 out of 10	70%
4. 8 out of 20	40%
5. 13 out of 20	65%
6. 17 out of 20	85%

Bonus: Shade one square and 17 out of 20 of another.
185% = 100% + 85%

What's the Percent? II
Page 14

1. 3 out of 5	60%
2. 1 out of 5	20%
3. 5 out of 25	20%
4. 17 out of 25	68%
5. 20 out of 50	40%
6. 35 out of 50	70%

Bonus: Shade one square and 35 out of 50 of another.
170% = 100% + 70%

Finding the Percent of a Number
Page 16

1. 20 squares	2 out of 10	2
2. 60 squares	12 out of 20	12
3. 35 squares	7 out of 20	7
4. 40 squares	2 out of 5	2
5. 20 squares	5 out of 25	5
6. 46 squares	23 out of 50	23

Bonus: Shade one 100-unit grid and 20 squares of another.
30 out of 25   25 + 5   30

Plate Circle Graphs   Page 19

Answers vary.
Ratio of Color 1 to Color 2 is the reciprocal of the
Ratio of Color 2 to Color 1.
Ratio of Color 1 to All + Ratio of Color 2 to All = 1.
Percents total 100%

Circle Graphs I   Page 21

Answers are estimates.

1. A. 25%   2. A. 10%
   B. 12½%   B. 25%
   C. 12½%   C. 25%
   D. 50%   D. 40%
3. A. 17%   4. A. 20%
   B. 17%   B. 10%
   C. 17%   C. 20%
   D. 17%   D. 20%
   E. 32%   E. 30%
5. A. 5%   6. A. 5%
   B. 20%   B. 15%
   C. 30%   C. 30%
   D. 45%   D. 50%

Circle Graphs II   Page 22

Check student graphs

1. A. 30%   2. D. 45%
   B. 40%   C. 30%
   C. 20%   F. 15%
   D. 10%   H. 10%

3. R. 32%   4. O. 56%
   T. 20%   A. 20%
   F. 16%   G. 15%
   C. 12%   P. 6%
   S. 20%   B. 3%

Bar Graphs into Circle Graphs   Page 24

Answers vary.

Bar Graphs and Circle Graphs   Page 26

#2, 5, 6 are circle graphs
#1, 3, 4 are bar graphs
Check student graphs.

Variable Percent   Page 28

1.-4. Check number lines
5. 45-50%
6. 10-15%
7. 60-70%
8. 90-95%
9.-12. Check number lines

Ladder Bars and Proportions   Page 31

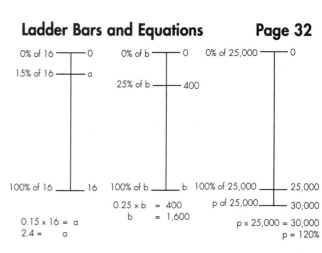

$$\frac{60}{100} = \frac{a}{95}$$
$$57 = a$$

$$\frac{35}{100} = \frac{42}{b}$$
$$b = 120$$

$$\frac{p}{100} = \frac{24}{64}$$
$$p = 37\tfrac{1}{2}\%$$

Ladder Bars and Equations   Page 32

$$0.15 \times 16 = a$$
$$2.4 = a$$

$$0.25 \times b = 400$$
$$b = 1{,}600$$

$$p \times 25{,}000 = 30{,}000$$
$$p = 120\%$$

Percents as Proportions   Page 35

1. 80/100 = a/40
   a = 32
2. 12½/100 = a/72
   a = 9
3. 50/100 = 33/b
   b = 66
4. 200/100 = 60/b
   b = 30
5. P/100 = 75/250
   P = 30%

6. $P/100 = 90/30$
   $P = 300\%$
7. $5.5/100 = a/950$
   $a = \$52.25$
8. $P/100 = 30/750$
   $P = 4\%$
9. $6/100 = 600/b$
   $b = \$10,000$
10. $P.100 = 900/27,400$
    $P = 33\%$
    3.3%

Percents as Equations   Page 37

1. $n = 0.65 \times 80$
   $n = 52$
2. $18 = 0.45 \times n$
   $40 = n$
3. $80 = n \times 200$
   $40\% = n$
4. $0.15 \times 80 = n$
   $12 = n$
5. $0.30 \times 90 = n$
   $27 = n$
6. $n \times 50 = 75$
   $n = 150\%$
7. $n = 0.15 \times 150$
   $n = \$22.50$
8. $7500 = n \times 125,000$
   $6\% = n$
9. $840 = 0.70 \times n$
   $\$1200 = n$
10. $34 = n \times 40$
    $85\% = n$

Let's Be Discrete I   Page 39

1. 2 items	2. 5 items
3. 1 item	4. 7 items
5. 9 items	6. 8 items
7. 3 items	8. 12 items
9. 8 items	10. 7 items
11. 9 items	12. 5 items

Let's Be Discrete II   Page 40

1. 2 items	2. 3 items
3. 9 items	4. 3 items
5. 1 item	6. 12 items
7. 3 items	8. 12 items
9. 2 items	10. 16 items
11. 18 items	12. 6 items

Percent Match   Page 42

1. B	2. E	3. C
4. A	5. U	6. S
7. H	8. D	9. N
10. O	11. !	

Because He Had No One!

Three-Way Match   Page 44

1. M	2. P	3. N
4. E	5. I	6. V
7. R	8. O	9. G
10. E	11. E	12. C
13. N	14. E	15. X
		16. I

Moving Experience

Get the Point?   Page 46

1. D	2. C
3. C	4. D
5. A	6. A
7. C	8. D
9. C	10. C
11. A	12. D
13. C	14. A
15. C	16. B

17. 1600.0
18. 4.500
19. 08.75%
20. 0200.

A Perfect Ten Percent   Page 48

1. 42	2	$2 \times 42 = 84$
2. 42	½	$½ \times 42 = 21$
3. $84 + 21 = 105$		
4. 7	8	$8 \times 7 = 56$
5. 7	½	$½ \times 7 = 3.5$
6. $56 + 3.5 = 59.5$		
7. 1.1	6	$6 \times 1.1 = 6.6$
8. 9	4	$4 \times 9 = 36$
9. 12	84	
1.2	8.4	92.4
10. 40	320	
4	32	352

All "About" Percent   Page 51

Answers vary.

Common Sense: Sense or Nonsense Page 53

1. S	2. N
3. S	4. S
5. N	6. N
7. S	8. N
9. N	10. N
11. N	12. N
13. S	14. S
15. N	

Let's Be Reasonable   Page 55

1. no   30% off would be $27 so the sales price would be $63.
2. no $100 - 20% = $80
         $80 - 5% = $76
3. yes $100 - 25% = $75
4. no   The rates are in effect for different times so they cannot be averaged.
         $1000 x 0.06 x ³/₁₂ = $15
         $1000 x 0.05 x ⁹/₁₂ = $37.50
         Total is $52.50
         $1000 x 0.055 x 1 = $55.00
5. Anne Gas costing $1.00 last year could cost $1.10 this year.
         1.10 = 110% x 1
6. no   ¹²/₁₀ = 20% increase
         ¹⁰/₁₂ = 16.7% decrease